Christmas
Concertina

Christmas Concertina
by Gary Coover

Copyright © 2013 Gary Coover

ISBN-13: 978-0615909660
ISBN-10: 0615909663

All arrangements and transcriptions by Gary Coover unless otherwise noted.
All scores and tablature by Gary Coover using Finale PrintMusic®.
Typeset in Constantia and Gabriola.

ROLLSTON PRESS
330 N. Rollston Avenue
Fayetteville, AR 72701
USA

www.anglotutor.com

Also by Gary Coover : "Anglo Concertina in the Harmonic Style", Rollston Press, 2013
                                  "Civil War Concertina", Rollston Press, 2014

Front Cover Photo: C/G Anglo Concertina made by C. Wheatstone & Co., Ltd.

All I Want for Christmas is a Concertina

My father asked me what I want for Christmas
A bicycle, a baseball bat and glove?
What I told him he found really quite surprising
Something to play the music that I love

Refrain:
All I want for Christmas is a concertina
The people love to hear its happy sound
All I want for Christmas is a concertina
So I can play my polkas all year 'round

My mother asked about this concertina
Would it be played or would it lay around?
I said that if I got a concertina
I'd learn to play and never put it down

Refrain

The years have come and gone now since that Christmas
I've played around this country far and wide
At times I think about that Christmas morning
And the gift that had my squeezebox stuck inside

Refrain

(Author unknown)

TABLE OF CONTENTS

THE AUTHOR / ACKNOWLEDGEMENTS

APPENDIX (for instruments with Jeffries accidentals, or if only 20-buttons)

INTRODUCTION

The Christmas season is a magical time of the year, full of good cheer, good food, good will and good music. With this book you can celebrate the holidays by learning your favorite Christmas songs and carols to serenade yourself, family and friends with your 30-button C/G Anglo concertina.

Although it may look like a little toy, the concertina is a highly portable self-powered music box that requires no batteries or electric outlets. It is easy to learn and to carry, and can make quite the joyous noise playing melodies and accompaniments. What better way to freely spread Christmas cheer?

There are many different kinds of concertina, but the tablature in this tunebook is designed specifically for the 30-button C/G Anglo concertina which plays a different note depending on whether you are pushing or pulling on it. However, the melody lines and chords of every tune can easily be played on any other concertina system or any other musical instrument.

Most of the arrangements are fairly simple and can be learned very quickly. Some will require a bit more determination and fortitude. Many use notes on all three rows of buttons on both sides, but don't worry, this book shows you which buttons you need for each tune. If you only have a 20-button instrument you'll be missing a lot of sharps and flats plus alternate notes – but you can probably still play most of the tunes with minor adjustments.

If you'd like to hear the arrangements and also see how they're played, simply scan the code on each page and you will be instantly directed to a YouTube video of the tune played twice through.

Of course, none of the arrangements are "definitive" – you are encouraged to embellish, adapt and revise as you wish to craft your own unique versions of these beautiful and timeless holiday classics.

So here is your Christmas present – 50 favorite Christmas carols and seasonal songs arranged with harmonies and chords, using the easiest tablature system yet for playing the Anglo. If you want to play just the melody, that's ok too, but an Anglo at full steam is the perfect way to make that joyful noise that will deck the halls, keep the home fires burning, drive the cold winter away, and make all your holiday dreams come true. It's now up to you to make all that happen!

Happy holidays!

KEYBOARD

The buttons and corresponding notes on the 30-button C/G Anglo concertina are arranged in a somewhat logical system, even if it is a bit confusing at first with two different notes for each button.

The middle row notes are the key of C and the bottom row notes are the key of G. The top row has alternate notes plus extra sharps and flats. The most common arrangement of the top row is known as "Wheatstone/Lachenal" accidentals. If you have a "Jeffries" instrument, the left hand side is the exactly the same, but 8 out of 10 notes on the right hand side top row will be different, so you may have to make some adjustments to the melody or the chords.

Notes lower in pitch are on the left side of the instrument and higher notes are on the right. In this graphic the notes shown on top of the line are on the push, notes shown below the line are on the pull. Standard abc notation has been used to show the pitches of the notes.

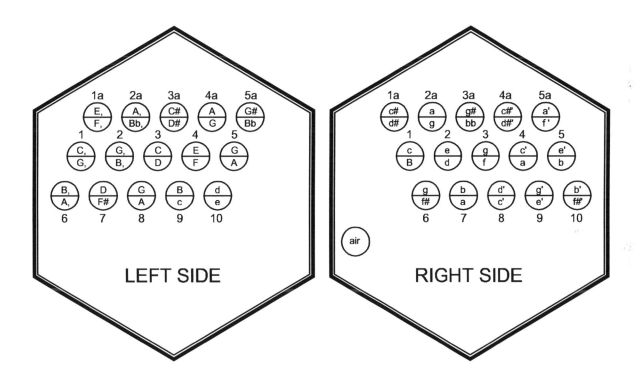

The top row buttons are numbered differently than the other two rows because they ARE different, and are not a normal scale in a particular key.

The third row is numbered 1a-5a on both side so when you see that little "a" after a button number you know immediately that you're up in the accidental/alternate row.

TABLATURE

This easy tablature system for Anglo concertina will allow you to play the melody and accompaniment for every tune in this book whether you can read music or not. Even if your concertina is not in the key of C/G you can still play all the tunes – they will just be pitched higher or lower than what is written.

How the tablature works:

- ◆ The buttons are numbered using the "1a-10" numbering system for each side.

- ◆ Notes for buttons on the right hand side are shown above the musical notes.

- ◆ Notes for buttons on the left hand side are shown below the musical notes.

- ◆ Notes on the push are shown by button number only.

- ◆ Notes on the pull are shown by button number with a line across the top. Long phrases all on the pull will have one long continuous line above the button numbers.

- ◆ Notes that are held for a longer period of time are indicated with dashed lines after the button number.

- ◆ Chord symbols are shown at the top of each line of music.

EXAMPLE:

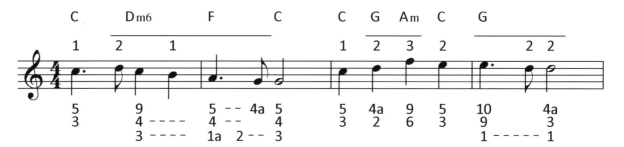

Additionally, to help you quickly see which buttons are required for each tune, look for a version of this graphic at the start of every tune:

Buttons played

TUNES

A virgin most pure, as the Prophets do tell

Hath brought forth a baby, as it hath befell

To be our Redeemer from death, hell and sin

Which Adam's transgression had wrapped us in

Aye, and therefore be you merry

Rejoice and be merry

Set sorrow aside

Christ Jesus our Savior was born on this tide

scan here for video

CHRISTMAS CONCERTINA

A Virgin Most Pure

Buttons played

English, c.1734

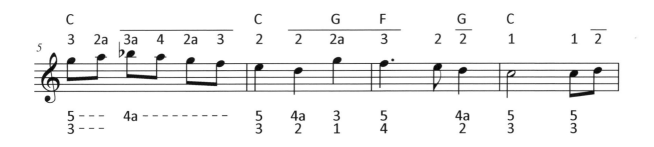

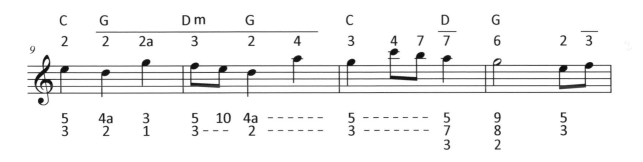

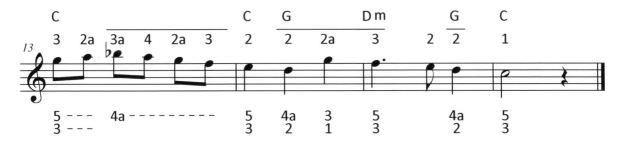

Angels we have heard on high

Sweetly singing o'er the plains

And the mountains in reply

Echoing their joyous strains

Gloria, in excelsis Deo

Gloria, in excelsis Deo

scan here for video

Angels We Have Heard On High

Buttons played

French (Languedoc) c.1800

Should auld acquaintance be forgot

And never brought to mind?

Should auld acquaintance be forgot

And auld lang syne

For auld lang syne, my dear

For auld lang syne

We'll tak a cup o' kindness yet

For auld lang syne

scan here for video

Auld Lang Syne

Buttons played

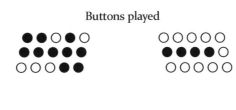

Traditional Scottish

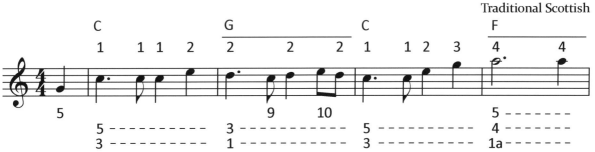

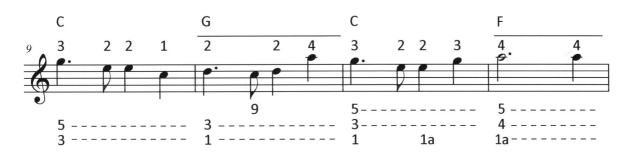

Away in a manger, no crib for a bed

The little Lord Jesus laid down His sweet head

The stars in the sky looked down where He lay

The little Lord Jesus, asleep on the hay

scan here for video

Away in a Manger (A)

Buttons played

Music: "Mueller" by James R. Murray, 1887

scan here for video

Away in a Manger (B)

Buttons played

Music: William J. Patrick, 1895

The boar's head in hand bring I

Bedeck'd with bays and rosemary

I pray you, my masters, be merry

Quot estis in convivio

Caput apri defero

Reddens laudes Domino

scan here for video

The Boar's Head Carol

CHRISTMAS CONCERTINA

Bring a torch, Jeanette, Isabella

Bring a torch, come swiftly and run

Christ is born, tell the folk of the village

Jesus is sleeping in His cradle

Ah, ah, beautiful is the mother

Ah, ah, beautiful is her Son

scan here for video

Bring a Torch, Jeanette Isabella

Buttons played

French, 17th century

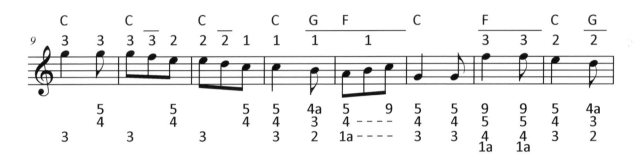

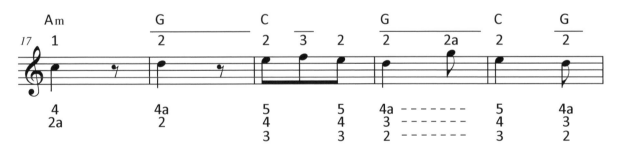

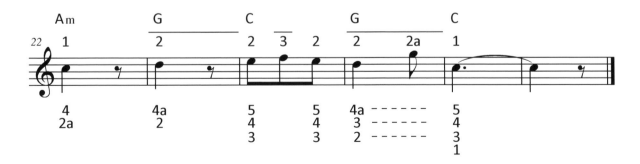

Lully, lullay, Thou little tiny Child

By, by, lully, lullay

O sisters too

How may we do

For to preserve this day

This poor youngling

For whom we do sing

By by lully lullay

scan here for video

The Coventry Carol

Buttons played

English, 15th century

Deck the halls with boughs of holly

Fa la la la la la la la la

'Tis the season to be jolly

Fa la la la la la la la la

Fill the mead-cup, drain the barrel

Fa la la la la la la la la

Troll the ancient Christmas carol

Fa la la la la la la la la

scan here for video

Deck the Halls

Buttons played

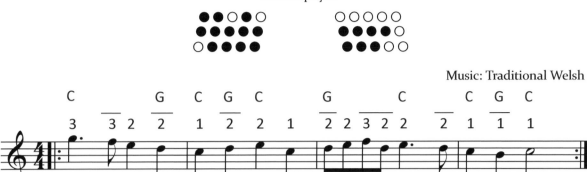

Music: Traditional Welsh

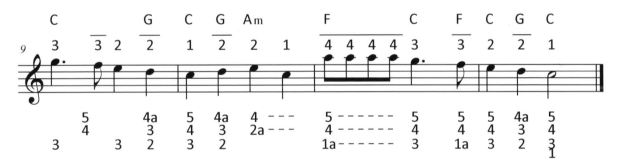

The first Nowell the angels did say

Was to certain poor shepherds in fields as they lay

In fields where they lay, keeping their sheep

On a cold winter's night that was so deep

Nowell, Nowell, Nowell, Nowell

Born is the King of Israel

scan here for video

The First Nowell

Buttons played

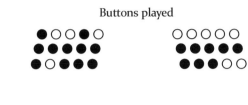

English (Cornwall), c.1823

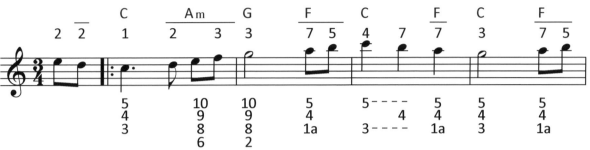

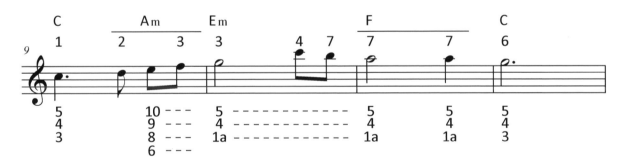

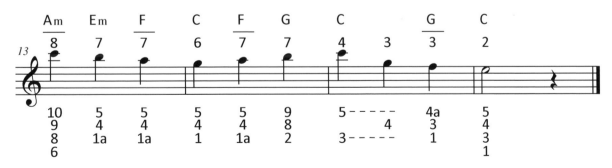

Gaudete, gaudete! Christus est natus

Ex Maria virgine, gaudete

Tempus adest gratiæ

Hoc quod optabamus

Carmina lætitiæ

Devote reddamus

scan here for video

Gaudete

Buttons played

English, c.1582

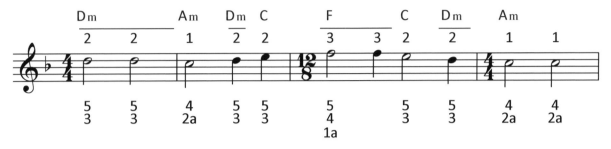

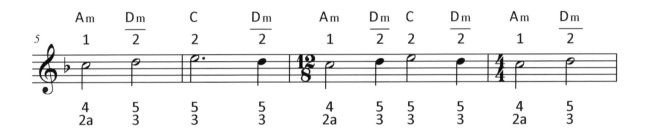

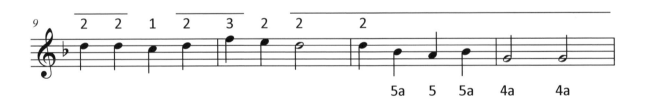

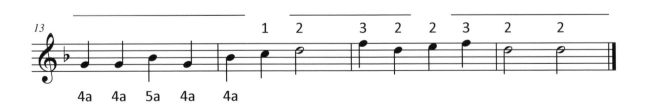

Wassail, wassail all over the town

Our toast it is white and our ale it is brown

Our bowl it is made of the white maple tree

With the wassailing bowl, we'll drink to thee

scan here for video

Gloucestershire Wassail

Buttons played

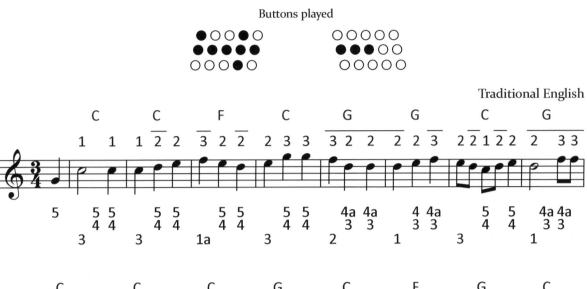

Traditional English

God rest ye merry, gentlemen

Let nothing you dismay

Remember Christ our Savior

Was born on Christmas Day

To save us all from Satan's power

When we were gone astray

O tidings of comfort and joy, comfort and joy

O tidings of comfort and joy

scan here for video

God Rest Ye Merry Gentlemen

Buttons played

English, c.1760

Good King Wenceslas looked out

On the Feast of Stephen

When the snow lay round about

Deep and crisp and even

Brightly shone the moon that night

Tho' the frost was cruel

When a poor man came in sight

Gath'ring winter fuel

scan here for video

Good King Wenceslas

Buttons played

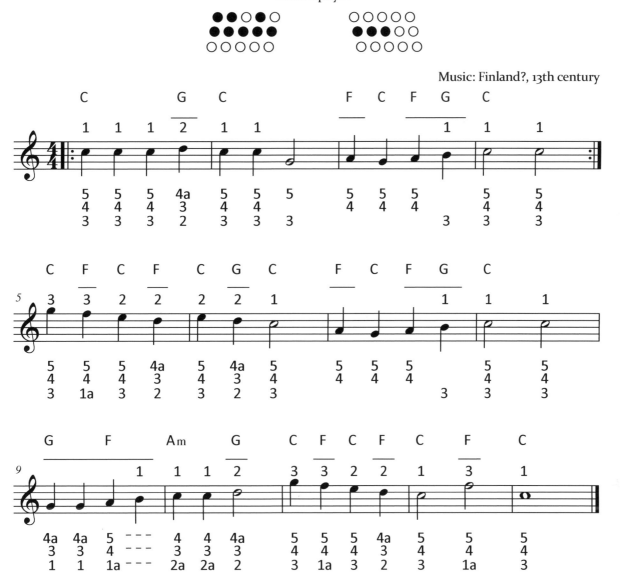

Music: Finland?, 13th century

Hark! The herald angels sing

Glory to the newborn King

Peace on earth, and mercy mild

God and sinners reconciled

Joyful, all ye nations rise

Join the triumph of the skies

With th'angelic host proclaim

Christ is born in Bethlehem

Hark! the herald angels sing

Glory to the newborn King

scan here for video

Hark the Herald Angels Sing

CHRISTMAS CONCERTINA

Here we come a-wassailing

Among the leaves so green

Here we come a-wand'ring

So fair to be seen

Love and joy come to you

And to you your wassail too

And God bless you and send you a Happy New Year

And God send you a Happy New Year

scan here for video

Here We Come A-Wassailing

Buttons played

English, c.1850

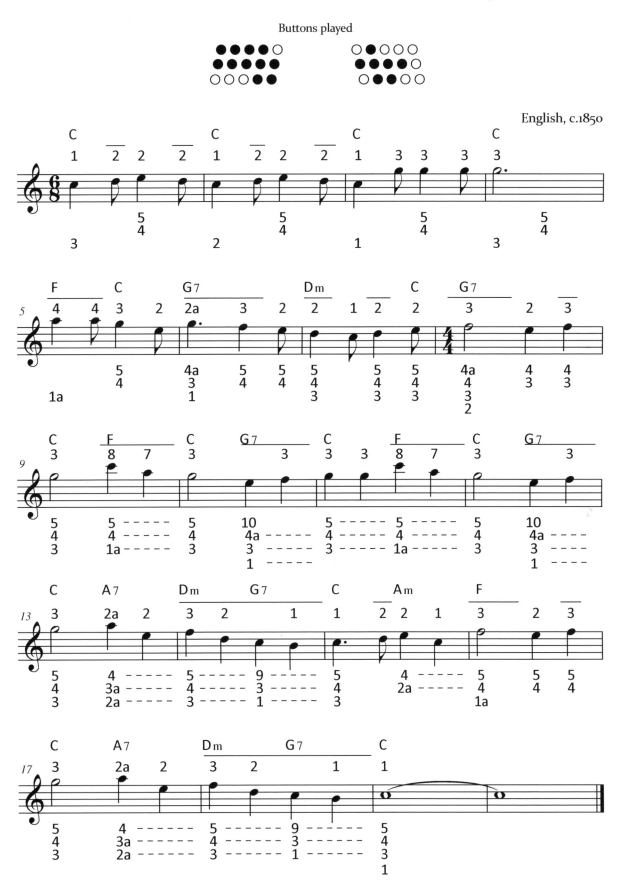

The holly and the ivy

When they are both full grown

Of all the trees that are in the wood

The holly bears the crown

Oh, the rising of the sun

And the running of the deer

The playing of the merry organ

Sweet singing in the choir

scan here for video

CHRISTMAS CONCERTINA

The Holly and the Ivy (A)

Buttons played

scan here for video

The Holly & The Ivy (B)

Buttons played

Traditional English

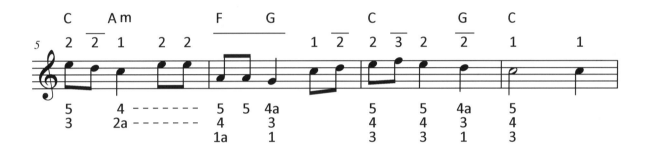

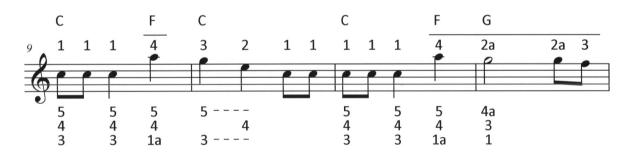

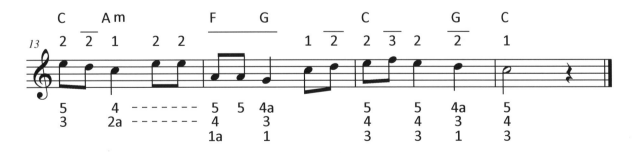

I saw three ships come sailing in

On Christmas day, on Christmas day

I saw three ships come sailing in

On Christmas day in the morning

scan here for video

I Saw Three Ships

Buttons played

English, 17th century

In dulci jubilo

Nun singet und seid froh

Unsers Herzens Wonne

Leit in praesepio

Und leuchtet als die Sonne

Matris in gremio

Alpha es et O, Alpha es et O

Good Christian men, rejoice

With heart and soul, and voice

Give ye heed to what we say

News! News! Jesus Christ is born today

Ox and ass before Him bow

And He is in the manger now

Christ is born today, Christ is born today

scan here for video

In Dulci Jubilo
(Good Christian Men Rejoice)

Buttons played

English, c.1400

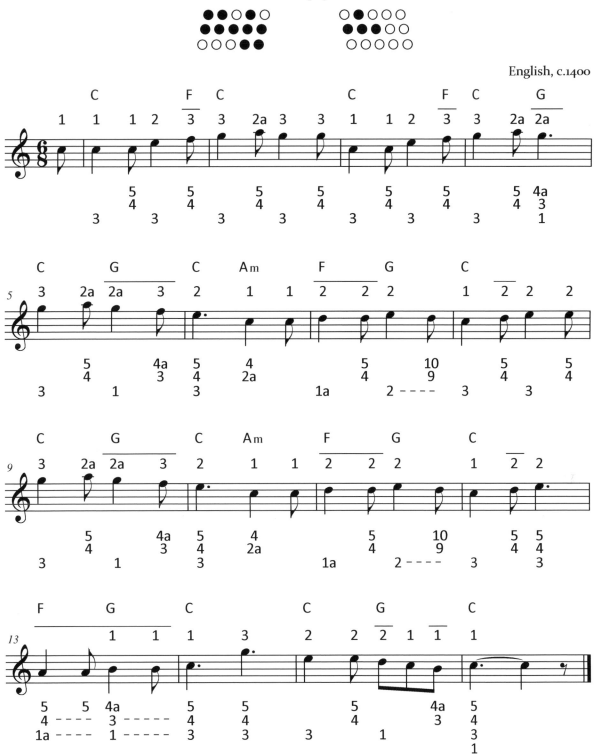

In the bleak mid-winter

Frosty wind made moan

Earth stood hard as iron

Water like a stone

Snow had fallen, snow on snow

Snow on snow

In the bleak mid-winter

Long ago

scan here for video

In the Bleak Midwinter

Buttons played

Music: "Cranham" by Gustav Holtz, 1906

It came upon a midnight clear

That glorious song of old

From angels bending near the earth

To touch their harps of gold

Peace on the earth, good will to men

From heaven's all-gracious King

The world in solemn stillness lay

To hear the angels sing

scan here for video

It Came Upon a Midnight Clear

Buttons played

Music: "Carol" by Richard S. Willis, 1861

At Jacob's well a Stranger sought

His drooping frame to cheer

Samaria's daughter little thought

That Jacob's God was near

Samaria's daughter little thought

That Jacob's God was near

scan here for video

Jacob's Well

Buttons played

Music: "Knaresborough" by James Leach, c.1790

Jingle bells, jingle bells

Jingle all the way

Oh! what fun it is to ride

In a one-horse open sleigh

Jingle bells, jingle bells

Jingle all the way

Oh! what fun it is to ride

In a one-horse open sleigh

Dashing through the snow

In a one-horse open sleigh

O'er the fields we go

Laughing all the way

Bells on bobtail ring

Making spirits bright

What fun it is to ride and sing

A sleighing song tonight

scan here for video

Jingle Bells

Buttons played

James Lord Pierpont, 1857

Jolly Old Saint Nicholas

Lean your ear this way

Don't you tell a single soul

What I'm going to say

Christmas Eve is coming soon

Now my dear old man

Whisper what you'll bring to me

Tell me if you can

scan here for video

Jolly Old Saint Nicholas

Buttons played

Benjamin Hanby?, c.1860

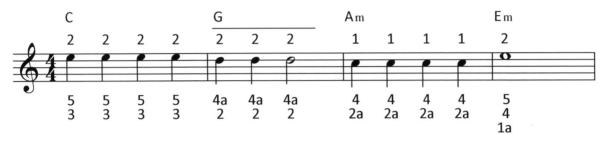

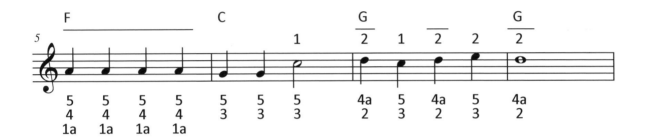

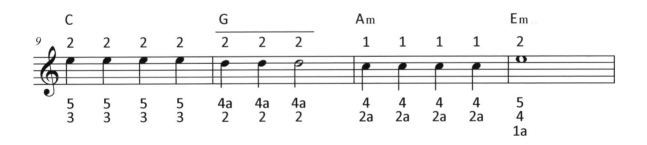

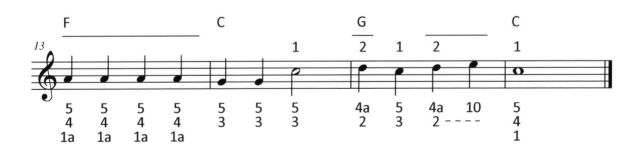

Joy to the world! The Lord is come

Let earth receive her King

Let every heart prepare Him room

And heav'n and nature sing

And heav'n and nature sing

And heav'n and heav'n and nature sing

scan here for video

Joy to the World

Buttons played

Music: "Antioch" based on "The Messiah" by George F. Handel, 1741

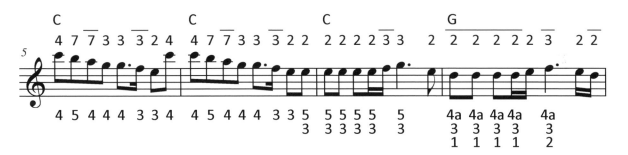

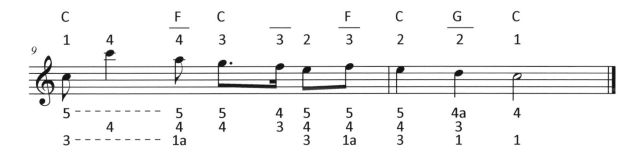

Joy, health, love, and peace

Be all here in this place

By your leave, we will sing

Concerning our King

scan here for video

The King

Buttons played

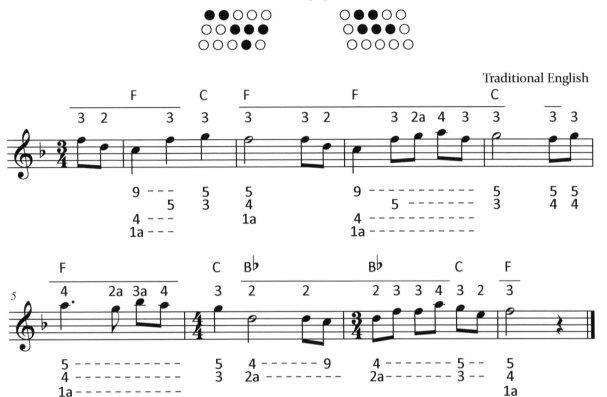

King Pharim sat a-musing

And a-musing all alone

There came our blessed Saviour

And all to him unknown

scan here for video

CHRISTMAS CONCERTINA

King Pharim

Buttons played

Traditional English

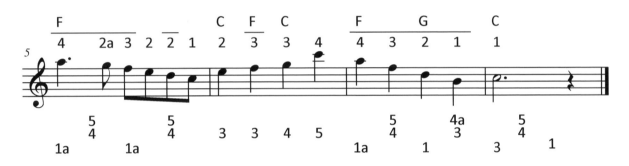

O Christmas Tree, O Christmas Tree

Your branches green delight us

They are green when summer days are bright

They are green when winter snow is white

O Christmas Tree, O Christmas Tree

Your branches green delight us

O Tannenbaum, o Tannenbaum

Wie treu sind deine Blätter

Du grünst nicht nur zur Sommerzeit

Nein, auch im Winter, wenn es schneit

O Tannenbaum, o Tannenbaum

Wie treu sind deine Blätter

scan here for video

O Christmas Tree

Buttons played

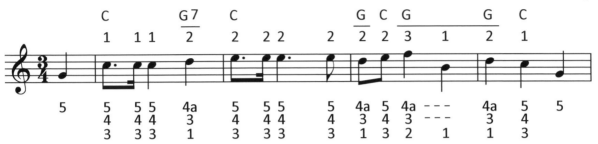

German, 16th century

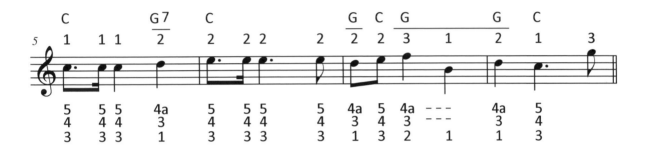

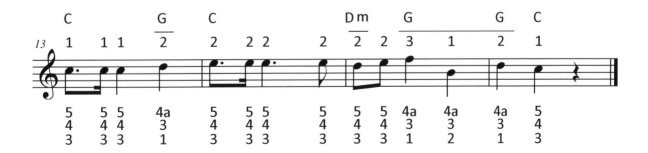

O come, all ye faithful

Joyful and triumphant

O Come ye, O come ye, to Bethlehem

Come and behold Him

Born the King of Angels

O come, let us adore Him

O come, let us adore Him

O come, let us adore Him

Christ the Lord

scan here for video

O Come All Ye Faithful

(Adeste Fideles)

Buttons played

English, c.1751

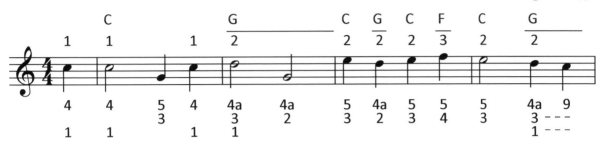

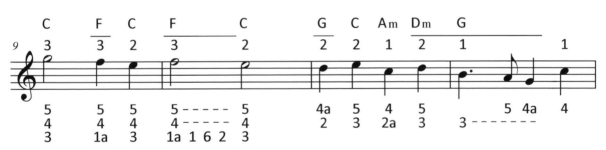

O come, O come, Emmanuel

And ransom captive Israel

That mourns in lonely exile here

Until the Son of God appear

Rejoice! Rejoice!

Emmanuel

Shall come to thee

O Israel

scan here for video

O Come O Come Emmanuel

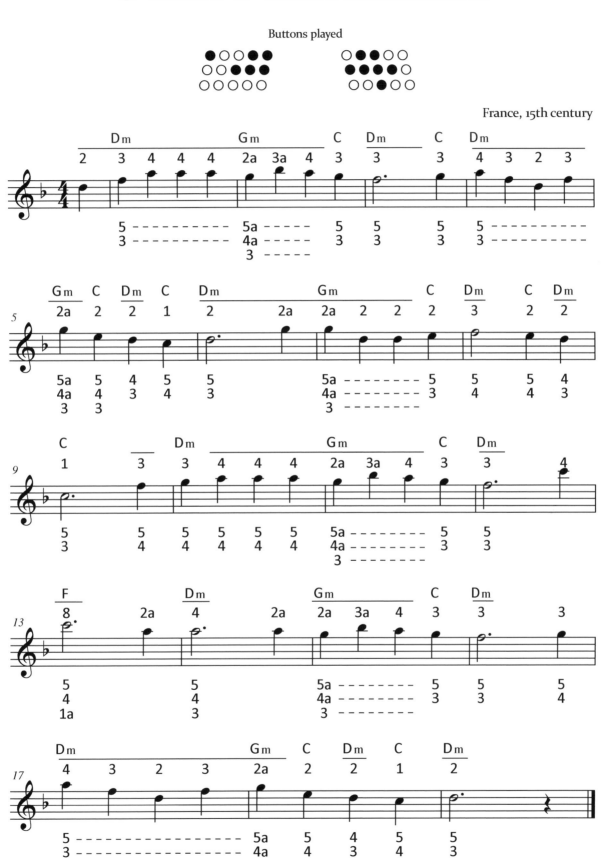

O little town of Bethlehem

How still we see thee lie

Above thy deep and dreamless sleep

The silent stars go by

Yet in thy dark streets shineth

The everlasting Light

The hopes and fears of all the years

Are met in thee to-night

scan here for video

CHRISTMAS CONCERTINA

O Little Town of Bethlehem

Buttons played

Music: "St. Louis" by Lewis H. Redner, 1868

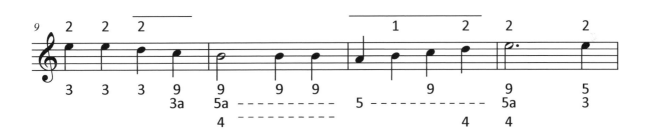

Once in royal David's city

Stood a lowly cattle shed

Where a mother laid her Baby

In a manger for His bed

Mary was that mother mild

Jesus Christ her little Child

scan here for video

Once in David's Royal City

Buttons played

Henry John Gauntlett, 1849

Willie, take your little drum

With your whistle

Robin, come

When we hear the fife and drum

Ture-lure-lu, pata-pata-pan

When we hear the fife and drum

Christmas should be frolicsome

scan here for video

Patapan

Buttons played

Bernard de La Monnoye, 1720

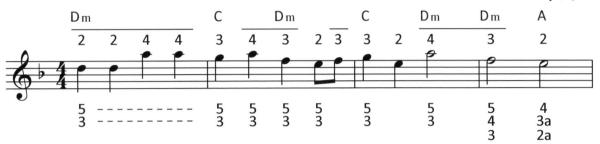

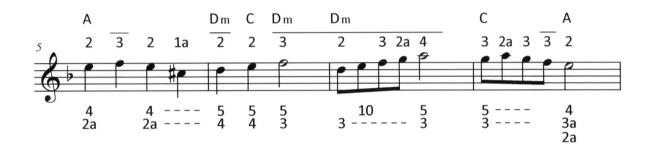

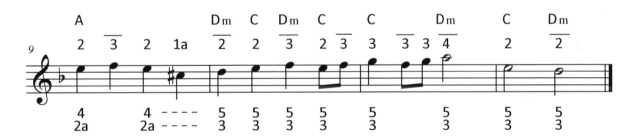

Now the holly bears a berry as white as the milk

And Mary bore Jesus, who was wrapped up in silk

And Mary bore Jesus Christ our Saviour for to be

And the first tree in the greenwood, it was the holly

Holly, Holly

And the first tree in the greenwood, it was the holly

scan here for video

The Sans Day Carol

(The Holly Bears a Berry)

Buttons played

Traditional English (Cornwall)

See, amid the winter's snow

Born for us on earth below

See, the tender Lamb appears

Promis'd from eternal years

Hail, thou ever-blessed morn

Hail, Redemption's happy dawn

Sing through all Jerusalem

Christ is born in Bethlehem

scan here for video

See Amid the Winter Snow

Buttons played

Music: "Humility" by John Goss, 1870

The very first joy that Mary had

It was the joy of one

To see her blessed Jesus

When He was first her Son

When He was first her Son

When He was Her first Son, Good Lord

And happy may we be

Praise Father, Son, and Holy Ghost

To all eternity

scan here for video

The Seven Joys of Mary

Buttons played

English, 15th century?

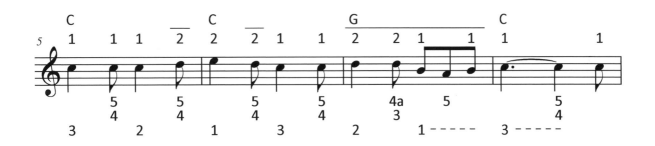

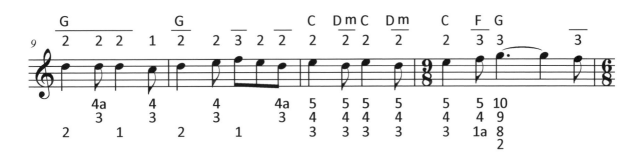

Shepherds arise, be not afraid

With hasty steps prepare

To David's city, sin on earth

With our blest Infant-with our blest Infant there

With our blest Infant there, with our blest Infant there

Sing, sing, all earth, sing, sing, all earth eternal praises sing

To our Redeemer, to our Redeemer and our heavenly King

scan here for video

Shepherds Arise

Buttons played

Traditional English

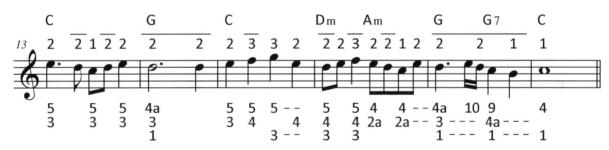

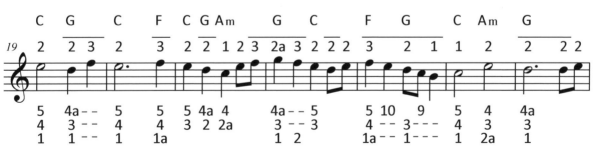

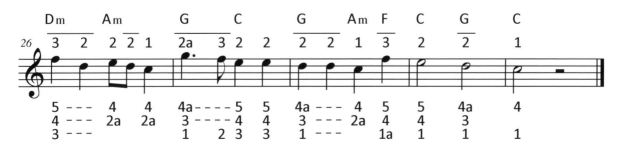

Silent night, Holy night

All is calm, all is bright

Round yon Virgin Mother and Child

Holy Infant, so tender and mild

Sleep in heavenly peace

Sleep in heavenly peace

Stille Nacht, Heil'ge Nacht

Alles schläft, einsam wacht

Nur das traute hoch heilige Paar

Holder Knab' im lockigen Haar

Schlafe in himmlischer Ruh

Schlafe in himmlischer Ruh

scan here for video

Silent Night

Buttons played

Music: Franz Gruber, 1818

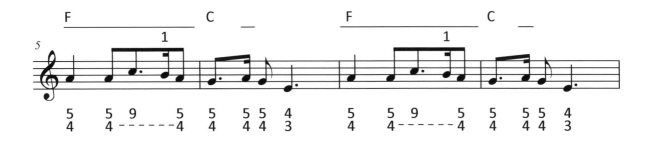

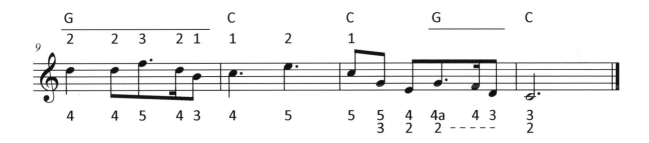

The snow lay on the ground

The stars shone bright

When Christ our Lord was born

On Christmas night

Venite adoremus Dominum

Venite adoremus Dominum

Venite adoremus Dominum

Venite adoremus Dominum

Venite adoremus Dominum

Venite adoremus Dominum

scan here for video

The Snow Lay on the Ground

Buttons played

Traditional English

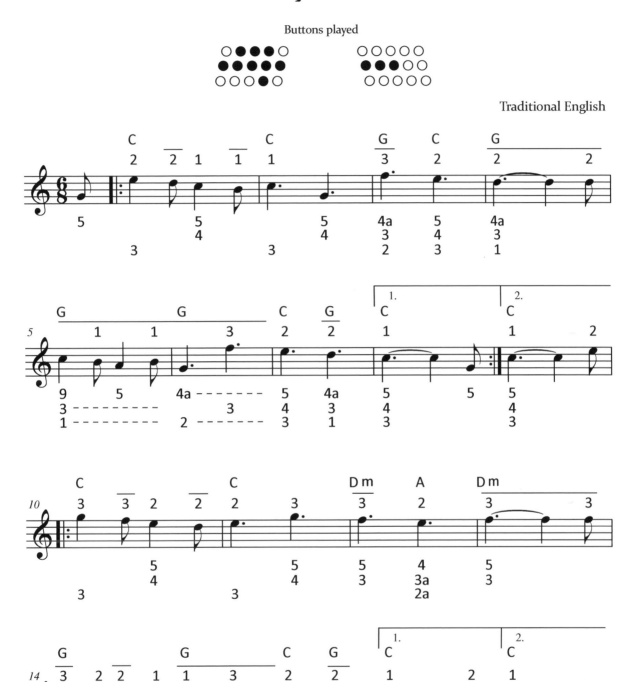

Wassail and wassail all over the town

The cup it is white and the ale it is brown

The cup it is made of the good ashen tree

And so is the malt of the best barley

For it's your wassail and it's our wassail

And it's joy be to you and a jolly wassail

scan here for video

Somerset Wassail

Buttons played

Traditional English

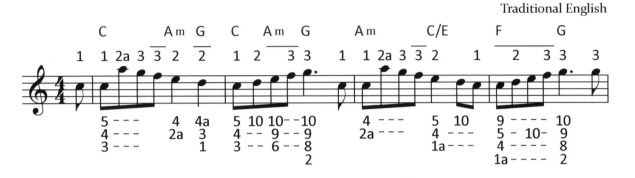

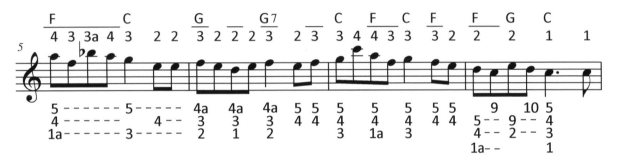

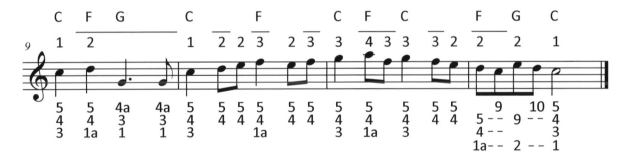

On Christmas night all Christians sing

To hear the news the angels bring

News of great joy, news of great mirth

News of our merciful King's birth

scan here for video

The Sussex Carol
(On Christmas Night All Christians Sing)

Buttons played

Traditional English

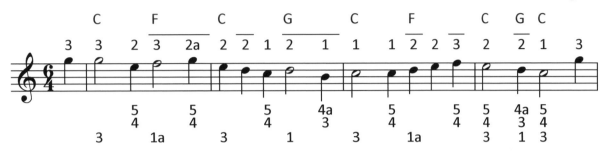

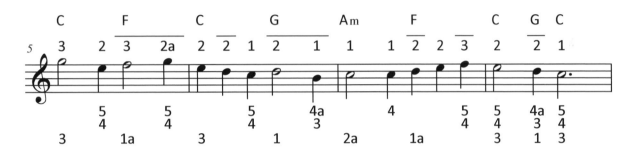

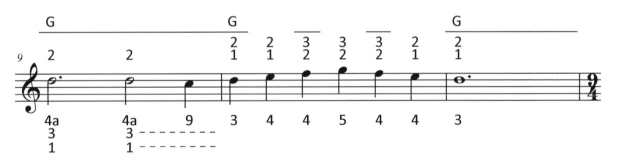

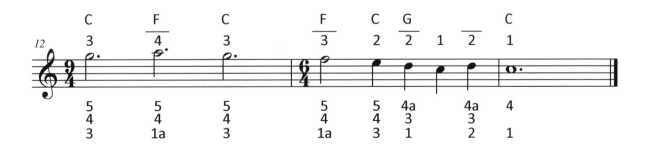

Tomorrow shall be my dancing day

I would my true love did so chance

To see the legend of my play

To call my true love to my dance

Sing, oh my love, oh my love, my love, my love

This have I done for my true love

scan here for video

Tomorrow Shall Be My Dancing Day

Buttons played

Traditional English

This is the truth sent from above

The truth of God, the God of love

Therefore don't turn me from your door

But hearken all, both rich and poor

scan here for video

The Truth From Above

Buttons played

Traditional English

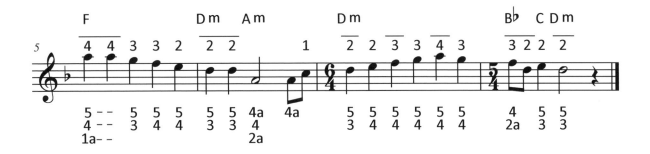

On the first day of Christmas

My true love sent to me

A partridge in a pear tree

Etc.

On the fifth day of Christmas

My true love sent to me

Five golden rings

Four colley birds

Three French hens

Two turtle-doves and

A partridge in a pear tree

Etc.

scan here for video

The Twelve Days of Christmas

Up on the house top reindeer pause

Out jumps good old Santa Claus

Down thru the chimney with lots of toys

All for the little ones, Christmas joys

Ho, ho, ho

Who wouldn't go

Ho, ho, ho

Who wouldn't go

Up on the house top, click, click, click

Down thru the chimney with good Saint Nick

scan here for video

Up on the Housetop

Buttons played

Benjamin R. Hamby, c.1860

We three kings of Orient are

Bearing gifts, we traverse afar

Field and fountain, moor and mountain

Following yonder star

O Star of Wonder, Star of Night

Star with Royal Beauty bright

Westward leading, still proceeding

Guide us to Thy perfect Light

scan here for video

We Three Kings

Buttons played

Dr. J.H. Hopkins, 1857

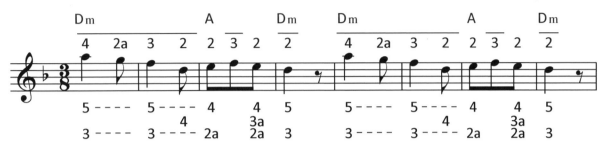

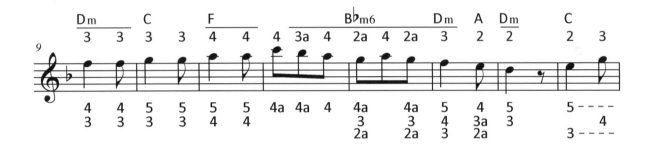

We wish you a merry Christmas

We wish you a merry Christmas

We wish you a merry Christmas

And a Happy New Year

Good tidings we bring for you and your kin

We wish you a merry Christmas and a Happy New Year

scan here for video

We Wish You a Merry Christmas

Buttons played

English, 16th century

What Child is this who, laid to rest

On Mary's lap is sleeping

Whom Angels greet with anthems sweet

While shepherds watch are keeping

This, this is Christ the King

Whom shepherds guard and angels sing

Haste, haste to bring Him laud

The babe, the son of Mary

scan here for video

CHRISTMAS CONCERTINA

What Child is This

Buttons played

Music: English, c.1580

While shepherds watched their flocks by night

All seated on the ground

The Angel of the Lord came down

And glory shone around

scan here for video

While Shepherds Watched Their Flocks

Buttons played

Music: "Winchester Old" by George Kirbye, 1592

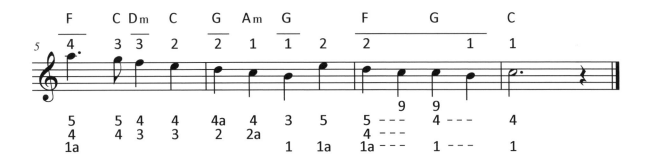

THE AUTHOR

It looks like the interest in squeezeboxes must have started very early one Christmas morning when three-year old Gary got a toy accordion for a Christmas present. Doubtless the noise he made with it at the time was anywhere near joyful except to him!

Years later he discovered traditional music via Steeleye Span and the "Morris On" LP, and subsequently bought his first Anglo concertina in a local music store.

Gary hosted and produced the popular "Shepherd's Hey" radio program of British Isles traditional music on KPFT FM-90.1 in Houston, Texas, for over 15 years, and his special Christmas programs were a highlight of the December holiday season.

A founding band member of The Four Bricks out of Hadrian's Wall, Gary played concertina, melodeon, keyboards and bass. He was also an original member of the Men of Houston Morris Dance team and played the "Egypian" King in the group's Christmas Mumming Play.

Gary has spent the last couple of years teaching and transcribing tunes for Anglo concertina, and is the author of "Anglo Concertina in the Harmonic Style", a 108-page tutor published in 2013 for beginners, intermediate and advanced players, and "Civil War Concertina", a 110-page book of songs from the 1850's and 1860's arranged for 20-button Anglo concertina.

ACKNOWLEDGEMENTS & THANKS

Special thanks to: The Oxford Book of Carols, The Open Hymnal Advent Christmas and Epiphany Edition, the Cyber Hymnal, and whoever wrote the words and music to the lovely concertina polka "All I Want for Christmas is a Concertina."

Videos of all the tunes in this book can be found on the "Christmas Concertina" playlist at www.youtube.com/angloconc.

APPENDIX

WHAT IF YOUR CONCERTINA HAS "JEFFRIES" ACCIDENTALS?

All the notes on the left hand side will be the same, but 8 out of 10 notes on the right hand side top row will be different. The right hand third row notes are mostly just shoved over one place to accommodate an extra d#/c# in the top left position. These are the Wheatstone/Lachenal to Jeffries substitutions you'll need to know:

1a ➜ 2a	2a ➜ 5a	3a = 3a	4a = 4a	5a = X
1a ➜ 2a	2a ➜ 3a	3a ➜ 4a	4a = X	5a = X

You lose three high notes: d#', f' and a'. But you gain the extra d#/c# plus a high d' (the "pull" alternate for 8 on the push). The "a" at **5a** is going to give your pinkie quite a workout!

WHAT IF YOUR CONCERTINA ONLY HAS TWENTY BUTTONS?

Some accommodations will need to be made, but you will be surprised how many of the tunes you will be able to play. The overall sound might be a little thin in places, and you might have to find new left hand notes/chords (or leave them out altogether) since you will most likely be changing whether you need to push or pull to get the right melody note.

First of all, fancy sharps and flats are out of the question. You have three F#'s on the bottom rows – **#7** pull on the left hand side, **#6** pull and **#10** pull on the right hand side. That's it.

Secondly, you have no substitutes for these third row notes:

Left Hand Side	**Right Hand Side**
— — — —	— — — —
1a, 1a, 2a, 3a, 3a, 5a, 5a	1a, 1a, 3a, 3a, 4a, 4a, 5a, 5a

Here are the substitutions you do have to work with:

Left Hand Side	**Right Hand Side**
2a = 6̄	2a = 4̄ or 7̄
4a = 5̄ or 8̄	2a = 3̄ or 6̄
4a = 5̄ or 8̄	

So, if your concertina is not a 30-button Anglo with Wheatstone/Lachenal accidentals, mark the substitute note numbers in the book in pencil and cross out the ones you don't have. If and/or when you get a different 30-button Anglo all you'll need is an eraser and a little time to retrain your brain and your fingers.

Made in the USA
Middletown, DE
04 December 2019